ROADS
SANTIAGO

A SPIRITUAL COMPANION
TWENTY-FIVE PILGRIMS SHARE THEIR JOURNEYS

Introduction

The pilgrimage to Santiago de Compostela

In 2006, around 100,000 people walked to Santiago de Compostela in north-west Spain, and every year this number increases. They take many routes following in the footsteps of pilgrims of the Middle Ages. The most famous route is the Camino Francés, a journey of 778 kilometres from the border of France and Spain to Santiago de Compostela.

Pilgrim reflections

In this booklet twenty-five members of the Confraternity of Saint James in the UK share their reflections on their pilgrimage with us. They do so to celebrate the 25th anniversary of the Confraternity in 2008, and hope their experiences will inform and inspire pilgrims and those interested in the pilgrimage.

The saint

James was a fisherman, son of Zebedee and brother of John. Legend has it that after preaching the Gospel in Spain, James (= *Saint Jacob* = *Sant Iago*) returned to Jerusalem and martyrdom. The site of his tomb in northern Spain was lost for some 800 years, when a hermit discovered the burial place. The relics were authenticated by the Church, and it became a place of pilgrimage which developed into the city of Santiago de Compostela.

In medieval times the pilgrimage grew in popularity. People set off from their homes and walked from all over Europe to Santiago. Religious Orders provided shelters along the way in which pilgrims could sleep, and cared for those who were sick or dying.

The priest and the paintbrush

The sixteenth century witnessed the beginning of a decline in the popularity of pilgrimage. Even in Spain, the once-great pilgrim roads gradually fell into disuse. But over the last forty years the Santiago pilgrimage has seen a great revival, especially in Holy Years (when St James' day, 25th July, falls on a Sunday): in 2004, for example, 180,000 pilgrims walked to Santiago. The next Holy Year will be 2010. Perhaps the biggest contribution to this revival came from Father Elías Valiña Sampedro, a Galician priest and scholar who, following the historical records, wrote the first guidebooks, created a chain of "Friends [Amigos] of the Camino", and from the 1970s onwards waymarked the many routes taken by the medieval pilgrims – by painting yellow arrows, approximately every 1,000 paces.

The modern pilgrim can follow the yellow arrows from Saint-Jean-Pied-de-Port in France all the way to Santiago, along the Camino Francés. Other routes include the Camino Inglés from La Coruña on the north coast where the English pilgrims arrived by boat; or the 1,000 kilometres from Seville in the south along the Vía de la Plata. These are only a few of the many routes!

The work of Fr Elías and Los Amigos del Camino de Santiago also helped build up a huge network of modern refuges for pilgrims, just like their medieval counterparts, and all along each route are "refugios" offering rest and sleep for a donation or a small charge of a few euros.

How long does it take?

As long as you want to spend! Some people set off from their own front door. Others choose a route and walk it in sections during occasional holidays.

Here are some examples of the duration of some of the many routes to Santiago:

Camino Francés, five weeks;
Vía de la Plata, seven weeks;
Camino Inglés, five days;
Camino Portugués (from Porto),
ten days.

The Compostela

Everywhere pilgrims stop along the way they obtain stamps on their Pilgrim Record as evidence of their spiritual pilgrimage. When this is presented in Santiago they may be awarded a Compostela – a certificate from the cathedral.

Pilgrim Record, with local stamps on its inside pages

Example of a Compostela

Pilgrim Routes
to
Santiago de Compostela

Scale
In 100 km units

© E Walker 2008

Angels

The roads to Santiago come from all parts of Europe; the scallop shell is recognised, far to the north, as the mark of a pilgrim. Coming from Calais, I was walking down the Roman road that connects Amiens to Paris. I entered a town that takes its name from that road, Saint-Just-en-Chaussée, and it was lunchtime. In a crowded restaurant, I ate, drank and called for my bill. "It's already paid, monsieur. Someone has paid for you."

The Roman road became a farmtrack. The first buildings of Greater Paris were ahead. A plump, moustachioed man leaned against his car and addressed me:
"Have you met him?" "Who?" "Jesus." "Not yet." "But you will?"
"Oh, I hope so! First St James, then Jesus."

Two angels to watch over me. The second was plump and moustachioed, but I never saw what the first one looked like.

William Griffiths

Pilgrim with Guardian Angel (stained glass at Pilgrims' Refuge, Tosantos)

For God commands the angels to guard you in all your ways.
With their hands they shall support you, lest you strike your foot against a stone.

Of the many stories about Elías – the inventor of "the yellow arrow" and rejuvenator of the Camino in modern times – this one perhaps captures him best. In Spain it is very well known; elsewhere, less so.

One day in 1982, with fears of terrorism rife, the sight of yellow arrows painted on trees along a Pyrenean road aroused the suspicion of the military police – the Guardia Civil. Following the trail, they came upon a battered white van. A small, smiling man got out. When prompted, he opened the van's back doors to reveal tins of bright yellow paint and a wet paintbrush.

"Identification!" barked the Guardia.
"I'm Don Elías Valiña Sampedro, parish priest of O Cebreiro in Galicia."
"And what are you doing with all this?"
"Preparing a great invasion…"

The rest – apart from the Guardia's reply – is history!

Laurie Dennett

The human heart may plan a course but it is the Lord who makes the steps secure.

My job as a guide-writer is to help the person using my book to experience the three component parts of any walking pilgrimage: poem, prayer and picture gallery.

For the pilgrim, en route, composes a *poem:* thoughts, reflections, a diary perhaps. The guide-writer concentrates, instead, on giving directions, describing monuments, accommodation, services. The pilgrim *prays* with his or her feet, a rhythmic rosary of steps, while the guide-writer measures distances, checks heights, terrain. The pilgrim walks through an ever-changing *picture gallery* of landscapes, people, places, pausing to admire significant "paintings" in the exhibition. The guide-writer, on the other hand, identifies landmarks, reference points, to help the pilgrim find his or her way.

Our undertaking is different, but we travel the same road, mutually supportive, mutually grateful.

Alison Raju

I will go with thee and be thy guide,
In thy most need to go by thy side.

Prayer

A pilgrimage is a journey to a holy place and one of its essentials is prayer. Without prayer it is only a long journey, however well intentioned. The original members of the Confraternity who met in London in 1983 had travelled to Santiago by foot, bicycle, car and train, and subsequent members have also gone on horseback, by coach or air. Any method of travel can count as a pilgrimage if the pilgrims have prayed along the way.

Eleventh-century church of Sensacq (Le Puy route, S. France)

Prayer includes the singing of hymns and pilgrim songs and since 1990 the Confraternity has had its own choir. Its members have raised much money for charities and sung in many places, including outside Santiago Cathedral at midnight, and on other occasions joining the congregation there to accompany the Botafumeiro* on its heavenward journey.

Eleventh-century church of Saint Pierre-de-Bessuéjouls (Le Puy route)

* A giant censer swung in Santiago Cathedral – see also p. 25.   Mary Remnant

Mondoñedo at dawn (Camino del Norte)

Cruz de Hierro at dawn (Camino Francés)

Who would true valour see,
Let him come hither;
One here will constant be,
Come wind, come weather.
There's no discouragement
Shall make him once relent
His first avowed intent,
To be a pilgrim.

Whoso beset him round
With dismal stories
Do but themselves confound;
His strength the more is.
No lion can him fright,
He'll with a giant fight,
But he will have a right
To be a pilgrim.

Hobgoblin nor foul fiend
Can daunt his spirit:
He knows he at the end
Shall life inherit.
Then fancies fly away,
He'll fear not what men say,
He'll labour night and day
To be a pilgrim.

from John Bunyan, *Pilgrim's Progress,* 1678

Setting out

I set out from Victoria station with several large bags. On the same coach to Spain was an Algerian, wailing and protesting, because the driver refused to allow her on with hens and multiple enormous bags. These she had to leave behind. I felt un-Christianly smug; I did not travel like that!

By early next morning, at Bordeaux, I realised (wailing and protesting) that I also was carrying too much. I had to shed not only the obvious extraneous kilograms of kit, but more essentially the unnecessary flotsam of my life – that erroneous conviction that *my* baggage (physical and moral) was more important and more "under control" than my neighbour's.

To move forward successfully, I first needed to sort out what to leave behind.

Gosia Brykczynska

Do not be worried about your life, as to what you will eat or what you will drink; nor for your body, as to what you will put on. Is not life more than food, and the body more than clothing?

From St Patrick to St James

Inspired by a TV programme and book, *Pilgrimage to Santiago* by Edwin Mullins, I set off to walk from Canterbury on St Patrick's Day 1982. I didn't have a proper pack, or waterproofs, or boots. I had two maps – one of France, one of Spain. I also took the Mullins book weighing 625g.

I found no waymarks until I reached the Pyrenees. There was little accommodation for pilgrims. Mlle Warcollier gave me a few addresses, one of which turned out to be a château! The first fellow pilgrims I met were cyclists Wolfgang and Josef near Pamplona.

I reached Santiago safe and sound on 22nd July.

Jocelyn Rix

Above Honto, crossing the Pyrenees on the Route Napoléon

May the road rise to meet you:
May the wind be always at your back,
The sun shine warm upon your face,
The rain fall soft upon your fields,
And until we meet again
may God hold you in the palm of his hand.

Cycling for St James

It all started in 1985 when I made the first of five pilgrimages to Santiago. I set off from my home in Dulwich on that occasion; later, from different places in France. I always cycled by myself – from choice – but I never felt "alone", making lifelong friendships along the way. My journeys were all very different and each had its own challenges and difficulties. I always tried to keep St James in mind, with the hazards he must have faced bringing the Gospel to Spain.

As I cycled I saw the seasons change and I realised there were times in my life to be at home and times when I had to journey to the tomb of the saint.

James Maple

The climb up to O Cebreiro, Galician border (Camino Francés)

To everything there is a season, and a time to every purpose under the heaven;
A time to be born, and a time to die; a time to plant, and a time to pluck up that which is planted;
A time to kill, and a time to heal; a time to break down, a time to build up;
A time to weep, and a time to laugh; a time to mourn, and a time to dance;
A time to cast away stones, and a time to gather stones together;
A time to embrace, and a time to refrain from embracing;
A time to get, and a time to lose; a time to keep, and a time to cast away;
A time to rend, and a time to sow; a time to keep silence, and a time to speak;
A time to love, and a time to hate; a time of war and a time of peace.

Pilgrim riders

Sisters Susie Gray and Mefo Phillips rode their Appaloosa horses, Apollo and Leo, leaving Canterbury Cathedral on 8th April and arriving in Santiago de Compostela on 15th August 2002.

We rode our spotted horses along the verdant byways of France and the wide golden landscape of Spain. And each day took care of itself. Brisk departures, bridles jingling. Midday breaks on flower-strewn hillsides and slow pacing to the day's ending. Horses first – food, water and a safe pasture. Supper, wine and laughter for us, and dreamless sleep.

The infinite kindness of strangers, the rhythm of prayer to a horse's hoof beats, the sense of belonging to this brotherhood of pilgrims making their way through the centuries over the worn stones of the Camino. These things will stay with me always. Thank you St James.

Susie Gray

Take therefore no thought for the morrow; for the morrow shall take thought for the things of itself.

Miracles at Montes de Oca

A tiny black and white kitten, skinny with hunger and thirst, was following us up the stony track, faintly mewing. In the shadow of some stunted trees, we sat to share our food and water, our new companion lapping gratefully from a makeshift saucer. We tried to carry the kitten onwards with us, but reluctantly had to leave it behind, in shade and with water, praying that somehow it would be rescued.

Later, at San Juan, we related the tale to other pilgrims. A German at the next table pointed and said: "But the kitten is there!" And so it was, to our amazement. A friendly Brazilian, whom we knew already, told us that he had managed to carry it to this refugio where the hospitaleros had agreed to take it in.

So if you meet a black and white cat at San Juan de Ortega, you will know its early history as a pilgrim kitten.

Patricia Quaife

Montes de Oca – a pause for reflection

"For I Will Consider My Cat Jeoffry"
(from *Jubilate Agno* written by Christopher Smart between 1758 and 1763)

For I will consider my Cat Jeoffry.
For he is the servant of the Living God, duly and daily serving him.
For at the first glance of the glory of God in the East he worships in his way.
For this is done by wreathing his body seven times round with elegant quickness.
For then he leaps up to catch the musk, which is the blessing of God upon his prayer.

The boy with the football

How does a boy cope with the challenge of walking 1,000 miles? I set out from Le Puy with my son Tom a week after his 13th birthday to make the pilgrimage in memory of his mother who'd died five years earlier. On our sixth day, as we struggled in the heat through desolate woodland, we met a local who, hearing our goal was "Saint Jacques de Compostelle", dryly remarked that we'd not make it that afternoon.

But Tom seemed to manage by giving himself a daily goal – literally: he carried a football in a bag hanging from his rucksack and wherever we stopped would soon attract a small group of like-minded enthusiasts for a quick game. We became known as "the English boy with his football – oh, and his dad…"   Robert Gussman

Children playing in the street, Santiago

… I am far from home;
Lead thou me on.
Keep thou my feet; I do not ask to see
The distant scene; one step enough for me.

The Camino dissolved our sense of time and was our exodus from a way of life. We walked with uncertainty, adopting a patient pace. The florid freshness of late spring evaporated as the Camino threaded its way across endless Castilla. "Torre, torre!" proclaimed our tiny sharp-eyed son, pinpointing a distant tower or spire.

"You have an angel with you!" a passing pilgrim observed. The beauty of the Camino we shared through our son's curiosity and agile fingers. He picked tender almonds, hulled pinenuts, unfolded budding poppies, and scavenged wild strawberries. Each night he asked uncertainly: "¿Estamos aquí?" ("Are we there?") He set our pace, turned heads, scuttled around plazas. In refuges, wardens sensing his tiredness found us a quiet corner.

Robert Sellick

Martin at the refuge in Rabanal, ready to set off for the ascent to Cruz de Ferro

Let the children come to me, and do not stop them, because the kingdom of God belongs to such as these.
I assure you that whoever does not receive the kingdom of God like a child will not enter it.

Blessings

Having walked through France to Dax over several years, I was contemplating the possibility of walking along the Camino Francés. I asked a returned pilgrim what I should take and how I needed to plan. His advice was to set off, albeit well prepared physically and materially, and when I was on the route, I would become aware as to what was necessary for my existence. I did not then appreciate the comradeship and friendship, the times for quiet reflection, the joyous pilgrim Masses, the weather, and Santiago de Compostela – I do now and I give thanks to God for all these blessings. Tony Ward

Thankful

Father God, help me to remember that there are more good things in the world you have created than bad and more blessings in my life than difficulties. Help me not to dwell on what goes wrong but to appreciate what goes right. Open my eyes to see beyond myself. Please continue to support me through the challenges and let me appreciate the many gifts you have given me, great and small.

Anon.

As the sun set and the homing herds, bells gently jangling, raised golden clouds of dust, we walked into Azofra, in the company of a worker returning from his fields. Where he had a mattock across his shoulder, we had a rucksack: birds of a feather. It came home to me then that there is a surprising similarity between pilgrimage and open-air labour: the early rises, the daily routine, hours on the go, tiredness in the evening along with dried sweat – and the sense of a day's work done.

Francis Garcia

If a man has a hundred sheep, and one of them should go astray, does he not leave the ninety-nine in the mountains, and go to seek that which is lost?"

Moral de la Reina, in the province of Valladolid (Madrid route)

Mountains at the head of the Vallée d'Aspe, Pyrenees (Arles route)

The Lord's my Shepherd, I'll not want. He makes me down to lie
In pastures green; he leadeth me the quiet waters by.

My soul he doth restore again and me to walk doth make
Within the paths of righteousness e'en for his own name's sake.

Yea, though I walk in death's dark vale, yet will I fear no ill;
For thou art with me; and thy rod and staff me comfort still.

My table Thou hast furnished in presence of my foes;
My head Thou dost with oil anoint, and my cup overflows.

Goodness and mercy all my days shall surely follow me;
And in God's house for evermore my dwelling place shall be.

Pilgrims' shelter

"Giving something back to the pilgrimage by opening a refuge for pilgrims." A simple thought but it was thanks to the efforts of other pilgrims that it all came about.

Through the Confraternity in the UK contacts were made with Spanish counterparts and the village of Rabanal del Camino was chosen where there was a former priest's house which could be converted. And so in 1991 the Refugio Gaucelmo in Rabanal was opened. Over a thousand donations had been received and by 2007 shelter had been provided for 100,000 pilgrims. A second refugio is now under way at Miraz.

Thank you to everyone for providing these facilities for pilgrims.

Walter and Mary Ivens

Refugio Gaucelmo, Rabanal – pilgrims having their evening meal

For I was hungry and you gave me something to eat, I was thirsty and you gave me something to drink, I was a stranger and you invited me in, I needed clothes and you clothed me, I was sick and you looked after me, I was in prison and you came to visit me… Truly, whatever you did for one of the least of these brothers and sisters of mine, you did for me.

Seeking and finding

At the Alto de San Roque stands a large statue of St James, one of many of "Santiago Peregrino" along the Camino. I found myself being reminded of Jacob in the Old Testament, always on the move. Jacob feels God-forsaken, lying down to sleep in a lonely place, and then wakes after his vision. "God is after all in this place," is also a pilgrim experience. In our own weariness we realise God is, after all, subtly present. Mid-life I went on pilgrimage to seek fresh motivation in life and found it.

Paul Smith

So do not start worrying. Your Father in heaven knows what you need. Instead first seek the kingdom of God and what he requires of you, and he will provide you with everything you need.

Alpha and Omega

Wayside cross near Saint Jean-de-la-Blaquière (Arles route)

You are – the thread I dare not break,
the need I cannot fill,
the presence that I find, and seek.
You are my kneeling, my walking, and my rest,
the bread I hunger for, my ground
of prayer, my solitude, the wood
my ever-restless hand explores;
my journey's wholeness, the blessings
at the outset and the end;
the hands that cup, entreat,
and hold me, day by day;
the wheel that carries me
from arrival to departure;
and my journey home.

Howard Nelson

O Lord, you search me and you know me,
you know my resting and my rising,
you discern my purpose from afar.
You mark when I walk or lie down,
all my ways lie open to you.

O where can I go from your spirit,
or where can I flee from your face?
If I climb the heavens, you are there.
If I lie in the grave, you are there.

If I take the wings of the dawn
and dwell at the sea's furthest end,
even there your hand would lead me,
your right hand would hold me fast.

Tidal flow off Finisterre, 55 miles to the west of Santiago. This cape was long thought to be the westernmost end of the earth, and many pilgrims still travel there.

The two journeys

For me, pilgrimage involves not one journey, but two.

There is the obvious outward journey with the physical effort of walking with my rucksack, sometimes pushing my body to its limits and coping with all that the weather throws at me.

But there is also the inward journey, having space and time to discover what is really important in life, coming to realise that so many material things, that I once thought were essential, are not essential at all.

The outward journey leads me eventually to Santiago with its cathedral and shrine of St James. The inward journey leads to a deeper understanding of myself and into a closer relationship with God.

Ricky Yates

This is what the Lord asks of you, this, only this, to act justly, love tenderly and walk humbly with your God.

Wounded feet on the Pilgrims' Way
Bound to a promise.
Soon you'll walk wet streets,
Soon
Sit on a hard bench and wait for rations,
Enter the Door of Glory,
Saunter to the swing of silver!

Still
Soon you'll desire to be back
    on the rough road,
Longer than life.

Stephen Malone

The Botafumeiro, a huge censer, has been used for centuries in the cathedral at Santiago.
Each day there is a Pilgrims' Mass for those who have arrived from all over the world.

"From farthest east to farthest west my name is honoured among the nations and everywhere a sacrifice of incense is offered to my name, and a pure offering too, since my name is honoured among the nations," says the Lord.

25

The hug

"Give a hug to the Apostle," strangers cry as I pass. I eventually arrive at Santiago's shrine and, taking a deep breath, climb up behind the seated silver St James. My hug of gratitude encompasses all the people, known and unknown, whose efforts have ensured that I arrived safely after my 500-mile walking pilgrimage.

Later, in the narrow streets of the old town, I am surprised to hear my name shouted out. A friend has calculated my arrival date, waited for me to appear and now races towards me to give me the most enormous warm hug. No explanation, just a hug.   Marion Marples

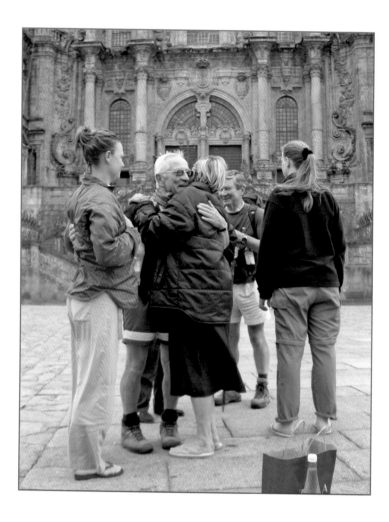

Most of us are pretty astonished when we feel love, and discover to our amazement that it's not like what we thought it was, nor how the films tell us it is. It is different; it is richer. It's very troubling and very chaotic. It turns our world upside down. It challenges many of our belief systems and our prejudices. But love also inspires the confidence to take risks with one another. You just don't know what trust in another person can lead to. And love is about courage. Do we have the courage to smile at somebody we meet for the first time, the courage to be friendly and warm, the courage to venture into unknown territory and encounter other people, with common sense and a clear, awakened mind?

Ben Okri, 2007

Arrés – a group of pilgrims watching the sunset in Aragón (Arles route, NE Spain)

Let us love one another, because love is from God ... Whoever does not love does not know God, for God is love ... There is no fear in love, but perfect love casts out fear. We love because he first loved us. Those who say, "I love God", and hate their brothers or sisters, are liars; for those who do not love a brother or sister whom they have seen, cannot love God whom they have not seen. The commandment we have from him is this: those who love God must love their brothers and sisters also.

To the kingdom

Being a pilgrim gave me a time apart from my normal daily life and I had the opportunity to look afresh at my relationship with God.

Walking the Camino gave me the chance to wonder at the glory of God's creation in both the people and the countryside.

My pilgrimage tested me both physically and mentally and I had a great sense of achievement when I reached the end. The sense of accomplishment and contentment remains with me today.

I realised when I reached the cathedral in Santiago that its majesty was but another waymark to the kingdom of God.

Stuart Goldie

Do not conform any longer to the pattern of this world, but be transformed by the renewing of your mind...

Our Father, who art in heaven, hallowed be thy name;

Thy kingdom come...

...thy will be done on earth as it is in heaven. Give us this day our daily bread;

and forgive us our trespasses as we forgive those who trespass against us;

and lead us not into temptation, but deliver us from evil.

Pilgrims yesterday and today

Researching the journey of the medieval Worcester Pilgrim for my book *The Cockleshell Pilgrim*, I faced many questions. What sort of Englishman would consider travelling through a continent ravaged by civil disorders? What really motivated him? Why walk, when many compatriots chose the sea journey? How did he manage from day to day, with sleeping, and eating? Who helped him? Whom did he remember with gratitude at journey's end? As I retraced his pilgrimage, it was remarkable how often archive materials agreed with surviving evidence on the ground, despite six centuries of change. Indeed, it was sometimes unnerving just how closely I identified with this man from the past, on our journey.

Katherine Lack

Give me my scallop shell of quiet, My staff of faith to walk upon...

The lessons

People often say pilgrimage must provide wonderful time for meditation, but sometimes my mind has run round in circles worrying where to sleep that night.

Pilgrimage has proved a journey into myself: testing my confidence in coping in a different environment, or my bodily strength and endurance – maybe dealing with being alone for a whole day and night. The benefits from this aloneness are being able to listen to birds singing and animals not being so quickly aware of my presence.

I have learnt how to ask for help or make a decision without being able to ask anyone else's advice. This is greatly because of the pilgrim experiences I have had.

Christine Pleasants

I asked for knowledge – power to control things; I was granted understanding, to learn to love people.

I asked for strength, to be a great person; I was made weak, to become a better person.

I asked for wealth, to make friends; I became poor, to keep friends.

I asked for all things, to enjoy life; I was granted all life, to enjoy things.

I cried for pity; I was offered sympathy.

I craved for healing of my own disorders; I received insight into another's suffering.

I prayed to God for safety – to tread the trodden path; I got lost and had to find the Way.

I got nothing that I asked; I am, among all people, richly blessed.

Anon

Room for everyone

Within days of starting our pilgrimages we met people of all ages from many different countries. We also found: some had prepared, some hadn't; some carried huge rucksacks, some almost nothing on their backs; some were shy, some outgoing; some believed in God, some didn't; some were happy, some sad; some had changed their lives, others liked life as it was. We met people who had lost partners, and couples walking with their children; some who had experienced broken hearts, and many who were falling in love with life.

We all walked the same road and when we got to Santiago Cathedral there was a place for each of us. Every one.

John Rafferty

Thomas the Doubter with Christ and the apostles, in the cloister of the Benedictine monastery of Silos, near Burgos (Camino Francés)

Blessed are the poor in spirit, for theirs is the kingdom of heaven.
Blessed are they who mourn, for they shall be comforted.
Blessed are the meek, for they shall inherit the earth.
Blessed are they who hunger and thirst for righteousness, for they shall be satisfied.
Blessed are the merciful, for they shall obtain mercy.
Blessed are the pure of heart, for they shall see God.
Blessed are the peacemakers, for they shall be called children of God.
Blessed are they who are persecuted for the sake of righteousness,
for theirs is the kingdom of heaven.

The spirit of the Camino

In early July 2000, I passed through Aachen on a millennial pilgrimage to Jerusalem, and attended a service in the great cathedral there. Afterwards, having seen the Camino de Santiago badge on my rucksack, a man came up to me and told me how he had walked from the Pyrenees to Compostela. Though we were complete strangers we both felt an instant bond. Since then, on three or four occasions on my way to Rome in 2004, I have had similar experiences and felt the same bond. This is not the least of the gifts that the road to Santiago gives to those who have taken it.   Mark Hassall

So we, though we are many, are one body ...

Roads to Santiago

Remembering, how we two walked
The roads to Santiago;
How simple was the life we lived,
How good the friends, how clear the way,
The feelings deep, the troubles halved,
A milestone on the road of life,
So many miles that stay with us
Those roads to Santiago.

It's true, it changed so many things,
It made us care in different ways,
We shared that life, it made us new;
Camino then, Camino now
Remembering still, how we two walked
The roads to Santiago.

Cristina and Paul Spink

Love is patient and kind;
It is not jealous, conceited or
proud;
Love is not ill-mannered or
selfish or irritable;
Love does not keep a record of
wrongs;
Love is not happy with evil,
but is happy with the truth.

Love never gives up;
and its faith, hope and
patience never fail.

Love is eternal.

What to do next

If you are interested in making the pilgrimage to Santiago de Compostela please don't just pack a rucksack, buy some boots and a flight to Spain, and start walking! Lack of preparation can lead to painful blisters and joints, and make your pilgrimage less enjoyable than it might be.

The starting point in your planning should be the Confraternity of Saint James, 27 Blackfriars Road, London SE1 8NY, UK   Tel: (+44) (0)20 7928 9988
www.csj.org.uk

The Confraternity provides a wide range of services such as:
• publishing guides to many of the routes to Santiago
• "Practical Pilgrim" days, organised around the country, which provide a chance for prospective pilgrims to meet more experienced pilgrims to learn more
• on these days, and through the website and publications, advice on what equipment is needed and how to plan your route
• a bookshop and lending library, and a regular *Bulletin* to members
• promoting research, and providing a bursary to young people undertaking a study of the pilgrimage routes
• offering help to elderly, frail or disabled people who might otherwise be unable to undertake the pilgrimage.

The Confraternity also runs two refuges for pilgrims at Rabanal del Camino (León) and Miraz (on the Camino del Norte in Galicia). These are staffed by volunteers.

Not in the United Kingdom? There are other English-speaking pilgrim associations in Canada (www.santiago.ca), Ireland (www.stjamesirl.com), South Africa (www.csjofsa.za.org) and the USA (www.americanpilgrims.com).

Links to associations in other countries (e.g. France, Germany, Holland, Italy, Norway, Portugal, Spain, Switzerland) are available on the Confraternity's website.